MATH START-UPS

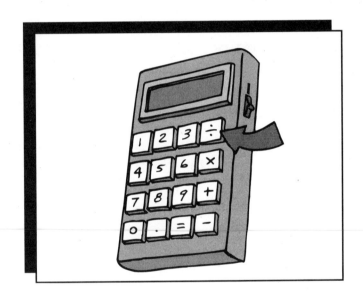

by
Scott McMorrow
illustrated by Philip Chalk & Marilynn Barr

Publisher: Roberta Suid
Editor: Annalisa McMorrow
Cover Design: Phillip Chalk
Design & Production: Scott McMorrow

Other books of interest include:
Thinking Start-Ups, Writing Start-Ups,
Web Start-Ups, Research Start-Ups

For a complete catalog, write to the address below:

Monday Morning Books
P. O. Box 1680
Palo Alto, CA 94302

Or visit our World Wide Web site:
http://www.mondaymorningbooks.com
e-mail: mmbooks@aol.com

ISBN 1-57612-114-3

Printed in the United States of America

987654321

Contents

Introduction

Math Start-Ups is designed to help students practice math skills while gaining knowledge of the world they live in. This is accomplished by providing basic math problems that relate to fun and interesting facts from real life.

The cards in each subject area (addition, subtraction, etc.) are numbered. In general, the level of challenge rises as the numbers get larger.

The math subject areas encompassed by the cards include:

Addition
Subtraction
Multiplication
Division
Geometry

An **answer key** is provided in the resource section, along with a reproducible "Student Activity Log." You can help students keep track of their progress by having them enter a card number into the checklist after they have successfully completed the activity.

Using the Cards

Icons appear on each card. These identify the mathematical operation being practiced:

addition   **subtraction**   **multiplication**   **division**   **geometry**

There are at least three effective ways to use these cards. For an **independent math center**, duplicate and laminate the pages. Some teachers like to use a separate color for each subject area: for example, blue for addition and green for subtraction. Cut the cards apart and place them in a shoe box or other container.

Give the class a brief overview of how the cards are structured. Remind students that the cards are numbered, and that the level of challenge rises as the numbers get larger. The reproducible "Student Activity Log" located in the Resources section will enable students to keep track of their efforts.

For **large group instruction**, simply choose a card yourself and copy it onto the chalkboard. You can then help individuals as the students work the problem at their desks.

At-home practice can be facilitated by having each student choose a card and rewrite it on a separate sheet of paper.

Number Whiz: A Math Play

This reproducible script, found in the Resources section, teaches math basics in an entertaining, read-aloud drama. The play can be presented to the entire class or done in groups.

Beyond the Book

Math Start-Ups is a "Web-extended" book. Questions, comments, and suggestions regarding the book will be published at our Web site:
www.mondaymorningbooks.com
You can e-mail us at MMBooks@aol.com, or send regular mail to:
Monday Morning Books
P.O. Box 1680
Palo Alto, CA 94302

ACTIVITY CARDS

1- Adding Oysters

Oysters are a type of mollusk that grow on oyster beds. An oyster bed can be natural or man-made. Man-made oyster beds are pieces of heavy string hung from wooden floats. These strings dangle in the water and oysters grow on them

Try this: A float has 6 strings hanging from it. On a single string, 20 oysters can grow. How many oysters can grow on the entire float?

Extra: An oyster farm is made of many oyster beds. An oyster farm has 15 beds similar to the one above. How many oysters can grow in this farm?

2- Georgia Peaches

Peach farmers need to know how big their crop will be each year. This information allows them to predict how much money they will make. One way to calculate the size of the crop is to estimate how many peaches will grow on one tree, then count the number of trees.

Try this: A typical peach tree might grow 118 peaches. How many peaches would a farmer have if she had 2 of these trees?

Extra: A farmer has 2 peach trees and wants to add another 2 trees. How many peaches will she have?

3- Red Kangaroos

Red kangaroos are the largest type of kangaroos. They can grow up to 7 feet tall and can jump as far as 42 feet in a single hop.

Try this: If a red kangaroo jumps 42 feet in a jump, how far does it travel in 2 jumps?

Extra: Imagine you can jump as far as a red kangaroo. How far would you travel if you jumped 3 times?

4- Moon Math

There are nine planets in our solar system. The chart below lists the planets and how many moons they have.

Mercury 0	Venus 0	Earth 1
Mars 2	Jupiter 16	Saturn 18
Uranus 15	Neptune 8	Pluto 1

Try this: What is the total number of moons for the planets Saturn, Mars, and Venus?

Extra: How many moons are there in our solar system?

5- Great Pyramids

The kings of ancient Egypt were called pharaohs. Three of these pharaohs built pyramids in an area known as Giza, near the Nile River. Below is a list of these pyramids and how tall they are.

The Great Pyramid of King Khufu: 481 ft
The pyramid of King Khafra: 472 ft
The pyramid of Pharaoh Menkaura: 218 ft

Try this: If you could place Khufu's pyramid on top of Menkaura's, how tall would they be?

Extra: If you stacked these 3 pyramids, one on top of the other, how tall would they be?

6- Whale of a Meal

Blue whales eat shrimp-like creatures called krill. One of these gigantic whales can eat 4,400 pounds of krill in a day.

Try this: If 2 blue whales decided to have breakfast, lunch, and dinner together during a day, how much krill would they eat?

Extra: How much krill would these 2 whales eat in 2 days?

7- Counting Cars

Traffic engineers figure out which street intersections need traffic lights. They do this by counting the number of cars that drive through the intersection. A busy intersection will most likely get a traffic light.

Try this: One day, 600 cars passed through an intersection. The next day, 750 cars passed through the same intersection. How many cars went through during the 2 days?

Extra: On Sunday, 1,000 cars passed through the intersection. The next day, 2,500 cars passed through. How many cars drove through this intersection on those 2 days?

8- Snow Pack

Snow in the Sierra Nevada mountain range of California melts each year. Much of this water flows into rivers and reservoirs and is used for drinking water. By measuring the depth of the snow, scientists can predict how much drinking water will be available.

Try this: During one year, 14 feet of snow fell in the mountains. The next year, 28 feet of snow fell. How much snow fell during the 2 years?

Extra: If 32 feet of snow fell in a year, and 22 feet fell the following year, then how much snow fell?

9- Picture Perfect

Photograph cameras use film to take pictures. This film comes in rolls and these rolls come in a variety of sizes. The number of pictures on a film roll is called the "number of exposures."

Try this: One roll of film has 24 exposures and another has 36 exposures. What is the total number of exposures these 2 rolls have?

Extra: Two rolls of film have 36 exposures each. How many exposures are there?

10- Making Books

Johannes Gutenberg is believed to have been the first European to print with moveable type. He printed his first book in 1436. He printed the Gutenberg Bible in 1455. Today's publishers use computers instead of moveable type.

Try this: A book publisher publishes 24 books one year and 28 books the next year. How many books were published?

Extra: A publisher publishes 45 books one year and 65 the next. How many books were published?

11- Alphabet Addition

A lot has been written about knowing your ABCs. Did you know you can add the alphabet as well? By assigning number values to the letters of the alphabet, you can add the various letters together.

Assign the following values:

A = 1,   B = 2,   C = 3,   D = 4,   E = 5,   F = 6,   G = 7,
H = 8,   I = 9,   J = 10, K = 11, L = 12, M = 13, N = 14,
O = 15, P = 16, Q = 17, R = 18, S = 19, T = 20, U = 21,
V = 22, W = 23, X = 24, Y = 25, Z = 26

Try this: Add the number values for the letters in your first and last name.

Extra: Add the number values for all the letters of the alphabet.

12- Mammal Math

Mammals are warm-blooded creatures that nurse their young. Mammals usually have hair. Types of mammals include whales, elephants, and humans.

Try this: Elephants have been known to live as long as 70 years. Humans have lived as long as 120 years. How many total years have the longest living elephant and human lived?

Extra: Killer whales can live as long as 90 years. How many total years would this type of whale and the longest living human live?

13- Letter Values

Long ago, people assigned a number value to each letter of the alphabet: A = 1, B = 2, and so on. Those who were superstitious favored words that added up to their lucky numbers.

Try this: Imagine that "determination" is a lucky word. What is its lucky number?

Extra: What is the lucky number for the famous words written by William Shakespeare, "To be, or not to be?"

14- Book Value

Bookstores have shelves filled with many wonderful titles that you can select from. The cost of the book is usually printed on the back cover.

Try this: Imagine you want to buy a book about sea animals and a book written by the playwright Martin McDonagh. If the sea animal book costs $16.50, and the McDonagh book costs $10.00, how much would you spend?

Extra: What if you also wanted to buy a book about nature for $9.95? How much would you pay for the 3 books?

15- Pizza Plus

When you order a pizza for home delivery, you have a variety of choices. You can get a small or large pizza, and you can request extra toppings. Remember, these things all cost money.

Try this: Imagine you order a small cheese pizza for $8.00 and a large, two-topping pizza for $14.30. What is the total cost of your order?

Extra: If you added 2 toppings to the small cheese pizza mentioned above, and each topping costs $1.50, how much would the pizza cost?

16- The Play's the Thing

Live theater has been performed since ancient times. Aristotle, in his book *Poetics*, made observations about the theater of his time. Many of these observations still hold true for today's theater.

Try this: If a ticket to one play costs $48.00, and a ticket to another show costs $62.50, how much would the 2 tickets cost together?

Extra: If you also bought a third ticket for $56.35, how much would the 3 tickets cost all together?

17- Toll Bridges

The fee collected for driving across a bridge is called a toll. Often, the money collected is used to help pay for maintenance and repair of the bridge.

Try this: The toll for crossing the Golden Gate Bridge is $3.00. If the toll for another bridge is $1.50, how much would you pay to cross both bridges?

Extra: If you crossed the Golden Gate Bridge once and crossed the other bridge twice, how much would you pay?

18- A Bevy of Bicycles

One type of bicycle, called "ordinaries" or "penny farthings," had extremely large front wheels and small rear wheels. Bicycles for two riders are called tandems. Triplettes and quadruplettes carry three and four riders.

Try this: How many riders could pedal on 2 quadruplettes?

Extra: How many riders could pedal on a bicycle, a triplette, and a quadruplette?

 MATH START-UPS © 2000 MONDAY MORNING BOOKS, INC.

19- La Tomatina

Since 1944, on the last Wednesday of August, the people in the town of Buñol, Spain, have had a special festival. From 11:00 a.m. to 1:00 p.m., everyone in the town gets together to throw tomatoes at each other.

Try this: If you could throw 225 tomatoes the first hour, and 198 tomatoes the next hour, how many tomatoes would you throw during the whole festival?

Extra: If you throw 423 tomatoes and your friend throws 387 tomatoes, how many tomatoes would you throw together?

20- Hungry Bats

Some bats eat fruit. Others eat insects. A large colony of insect-eating bats can eat 6,000 tons of insects in a year. A single bat can eat as many as 600 mosquitoes in an hour!

Try this: If one bat eats 612 mosquitoes, and another bat eats 546 mosquitoes, how many insects did both bats eat?

Extra: If one bat eats 5,654 mosquitoes, and another bat eats 4,817 mosquitoes, how many insects did both bats eat?

21- Tallying the Rain Forest

A typical patch of rain forest covering 4 square miles contains 750 species of trees, 750 species of other plants, 125 species of mammals, 400 species of birds, 100 species of reptiles, and 60 species of amphibians.

Try this: How many types of trees and plants grow in a typical patch of rain forest?

Extra: How many trees, plants, mammals, birds, reptiles, and amphibians grow in a typical patch of rain forest?

22- Using Hieroglyphics

The Egyptians used hieroglyphic script from 3100 BC until AD 400.

Try this: How long did the Egyptians use hieroglyphics?

Extra: If an Egyptian writer, called a scribe, was born in 3100 BC and died in 3054 BC, how old was he when he died?

Note: Dates with the letters BC after them refer to times before the year 0. With these dates, higher numbered years occurred in time before lower numbers. For example, 5,000 BC came before 2,000 BC.

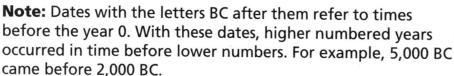

1- Jet Plane Planning

An pilot always needs to know how far the plane has flown during a flight. By knowing the distance travelled, a pilot can figure out how much farther there is to fly.

Try this: Imagine you are flying a plane from Los Angeles to San Francisco. The total trip is about 500 miles and you have flown 250 miles. How many more miles will you fly?

Extra: The distance between San Francisco and New York City is about 3,600 miles. If you have flown 2,512 miles, how much farther do you need to fly to reach New York?

2- Big Tooth

The largest shark that ever lived was the Great Shark, megalodon. Now extinct, this huge beast is an ancestor of the current-day Great White Shark.

Try this: Megalodon sharks grew to be as long as 55 feet. Megalodon's smaller relative, the Great White Shark, can grow as big as 26 feet. What is the size difference between these sharks?

Extra: Another big shark is the tiger shark. It can grow up to 20 feet. What is the size difference between a tiger shark and megalodon?

3- School Days

How much time do you spend in school? The average school year lasts 9 months. This equals about 180 days spent in school each year, not including weekends.

Try this: If a year is 365 days long, how many days does a typical student spend out of school?

Extra: If you took classes for 11 months (220 days), how many days would you spend out of school?

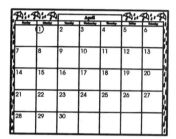

4- George Washington

George Washington was the first president of the United States. Did you know he also held various other jobs? During his life, George was a surveyor, military officer, and writer.

Try this: George Washington was born in 1732, and he became president in 1789. How old was he when he first became president?

Extra: George's wife, Martha, was born in 1731. How old was she when her husband became president?

5- Fishing for Math

Commercial fishermen go to sea in boats and try to catch large numbers of fish. To them, fishing is a full-time job.

Try this: Commercial fishermen are catching fewer fish each year. Imagine a fisherman who catches 5,613 fish one year and 4,276 the next year. How many fewer fish did that fisherman catch?

Extra: Imagine 9,010 boats went fishing this year and 8,238 went fishing last year. How many more boats went fishing this year?

6- Civil Engineering

Civil engineers design and build many things, including bridges, roads, water systems, and airports. A special license is needed to approve plans for such projects. This is called a Professional Engineer license.

Try this: During one year, 6,468 civil engineers receive a Professional Engineer license. The next year, 6,198 civil engineers receive this special license. How many fewer engineers were licensed in the second year?

Extra: In one year, 8,496 civil engineers receive a license and 9,234 receive it the next year. How many more engineers got their license the second year?

7- How Far?

The two places in the United States (not including Alaska or Hawaii) that are farthest apart are Cape Flattery, Washington, and the south coast of Florida. These two places are 2,835 miles apart.

Try this: Imagine a town that is between these two places and is 310 miles away from Cape Flattery. How far is this town from the most distant place in Florida?

Extra: Another town between these two places is 1,287 miles from southern Florida. How far is it from Cape Flattery?

8- Border Math

A border is an imaginary line that separates countries. The length of the United States' border with Canada is 3,987 miles. The length of the United States' border with Mexico is 1,933 miles.

Try this: How much longer is the Canadian border than the Mexican border?

Extra: How long are the two borders if added together?

9- Bug Out

A centipede has many legs. It gets its name from two Latin words. *Centum* is Latin for one hundred, and *pes* is Latin for foot. Based on the name, you'd expect a centipede to have 100 legs. This isn't always the case.

Try this: The greatest number of legs found on a centipede was 177. How many more legs did this creature have than its name suggests?

Extra: A millipede is another many-legged creature. *Milli* means 1,000, but the most legs found on a millipede was 375. How many more legs would this creature need to be a true millipede?

10- Mayor Math

The first black mayor in the United States was Carl B. Stokes. He became the mayor of Cleveland, Ohio, in 1967, and served as mayor until 1971.

Try this: Mr. Stokes was born in 1927. How old was he when he became mayor of Cleveland?

Extra: How old was Mr. Stokes when he left office?

Ohio

Red Carnation

11- Tall Trees

Some of the world's tallest living trees grow in California. General Sherman, a giant sequoia, is 275 feet tall. The Mendocino Tree, a redwood, is 367.5 feet tall.

Try this: How much shorter is General Sherman than the Mendocino Tree?

Extra: The diameter of General Sherman is 102.6 feet, and the diameter of the Mendocino Tree is 10.4 feet. How much thicker is General Sherman?

12- Lizard Length

Lizards come in different sizes, shapes, and colors. The largest lizard is the adult male Komodo dragon. These have been know to grow as long as 10.16 feet.

Try this: The smallest lizard is a tiny gecko that lives on one of the British Virgin Islands. This tiny lizard only grows to be 0.06 foot long. How much longer is the Komodo dragon than this gecko?

Extra: If the tiny gecko were 0.16 foot long, how much longer would the Komodo dragon be?

13- Big Birds

The tallest flying birds are cranes. These have been recorded to be as tall as 6.5 feet. The smallest birds are male bee hummingbirds from Cuba. These tiny birds only grow to be 0.18 foot long.

Try this: How much shorter is the bee hummingbird than the crane?

Extra: Ostriches are the largest non-flying bird and can reach 9 feet in height. How much taller is the ostrich than the crane?

14- Pinniped Problem

A pinniped is an animal that has fin-like feet or flippers. The largest pinniped is the elephant seal of the sub-Antarctic islands. These animals grow as long as 21.33 feet.

Try this: The smallest pinniped is the 3.9 feet long Galápagos fur seal. How much longer is the elephant seal than the fur seal?

Extra: How much larger would the elephant seal be if the fur seal were 4.79 feet long?

15- Swimming the Channel

The English Channel is the body of water separating England and France. Many swimmers like to challenge themselves by swimming across from one country to the other. The narrowest distance of the channel is 21 miles and the widest is 150 miles.

Try this: One swimmer swam the channel in 7.28 hours and another person swam across in 7.67 hours. How much faster did the first swimmer cross the channel?

Extra: Bertram Batt, at age 67, swam across in 18.61 hours. Susan Fraenkel, age 49, swam across in 12.08 hours. How much faster was Susan?

16- Oh Deer!

The Alaskan moose is the largest type of deer. Records show that one of these deer was measured as 7.67 feet tall. The smallest known deer is the southern pudu that lives in Chile and Argentina. This tiny deer only grows to be about 1.25 feet tall.

Try this: How much bigger is the Alaskan moose compared to the southern pudu?

Extra: If a person is 5.83 feet tall, how much taller is the Alaskan moose?

17- Noisy Monkey

The howler monkey makes a noise that sounds like a donkey trying to bark like a dog. These monkeys, which live in Central and South America, can be heard as far as 3.1 miles away.

Try this: Imagine you are standing 2.86 miles away from a howling howler monkey and your best friend is 2.93 miles away. How far apart are you and your friend?

Extra: Imagine you are 0.55 miles away and your friend is still 2.93 miles away. How far apart are you?

18- Short and Tall

A man and woman were married in France. The man, Fabien Pretou, was 6.12 feet tall. The woman, Natalie Lucius, was 3.08 feet tall.

Try this: How much taller was Fabien than Natalie?

Extra: The tallest man on record, Robert Wadlow, was 8.91 feet tall. How much taller was he than Fabien?

19- Deep in the Ocean

A bathyscaphe is a type of deep-sea diving device that people can use to travel deep in oceans. In 1960, two people used a bathyscaphe to reach an ocean depth of 35,797 feet.

Try this: It took 4.8 hours to reach the depth mentioned above. The trip back to the surface took 3.28 hours. How much shorter was the trip to the surface?

Extra: The total round-trip travel time was 8.08 hours. Based on a 24-hour day, how many hours remained in the day?

20- High Art

Vincent Van Gogh's painting, *Portrait of Dr. Gachet*, sold for $82.5 million. This is considered the highest price paid for a painting. An Edgar Degas sculpture, *Petite danseuse de quatorze*, sold for $11.8 million. This is the highest price paid for a sculpture.

Try this: How much more did Van Gogh's painting cost than the Degas sculpture?

Extra: The highest price paid for a book is $11.9 million. How much more was paid for the Van Gogh painting?

21- Floating Bridge

The Second Lake Washington Bridge actually has a section that floats on water. Located in Seattle, this 12,596 foot-long bridge has a 7,518-foot section that floats on top of Lake Washington.

Try this: Calculate the length of this bridge that does not float.

Extra: The Quebec Bridge in Canada is 3,239 feet long. What is the difference in length of these two bridges?

22- Moon Temperature

The temperature on the moon varies greatly in a single day. When the sun is directly over the moon's equator, the temperature reaches 243 degrees Fahrenheit.

Try this: Around sunset, the temperature on the moon drops to 58 degrees Fahrenheit. What is the difference between the daytime and sunset temperatures?

Extra: After nightfall, the moon's temperature drops to -261 degrees Fahrenheit. What is the temperature difference between sunset and nighttime?

23- Plant Lives

The highest-living plants have been found at 21,000 feet on Mt. Kamet in the Himalayas. The deepest-living plant was found at a depth of 884 feet in waters off of San Salvador Island in the Bahamas.

Try this: Calculate the difference in living heights of these plants. Remember that the underwater plant is really at -884 feet.

Extra: Mt. Everest, another mountain in the Himalayas, is 29,028 feet tall. What is the difference between Mt. Everest's height and the height of the plants on Mt. Kamet?

24- General Hannibal

Hannibal was a Carthaginian general who was born in 247 BC and died in 183 or 182 BC. He is believed to be one of the great military geniuses of all time. He is famous for crossing the Alps with a full baggage train and elephants. He traveled to Rome in 217 BC.

Try this: How old was Hannibal when he traveled to Rome?

Extra: If Hannibal died in 182 BC, how old was he at his death?

Note: Dates with the letters BC after them refer to times before the year 0. With these dates, higher numbered years occurred in time before lower numbers. For example, 5,000 BC came before 2,000 BC.

1- A Day on Mars

On Earth, a day is defined as a specific 24-hour period. Scientists have a special name for a Martian day. They call a day on Mars a "sol." A sol is 24.7 hours long, which is slightly longer than an Earth day.

Try this: If one Martian sol is 24.7 hours long, how many hours are there in a Martian week (7 sols)?

Extra: How many hours are there in a Martian year (52 Martian weeks)?

2- Bottom of the Sea

There are many different units of measurement. The second, minute, and hour measure time. Inches, feet, meters, and kilometers are used to measure distance. The depth of the ocean is often measured using two units, feet and fathoms. One fathom equals 6 feet.

Try this: Many types of ocean fish live in water that is 100 fathoms deep. How many feet deep are these fish?

Extra: Trenches in the ocean floor have been measured to be as deep as 6,000 fathoms. How many feet deep are these trenches?

3- Fault-Line Forecasting

Most earthquakes occur along faults or fault lines. An earthquake happens when the land on both sides of the fault moves quickly in opposite directions. However, this movement is always occurring, even when there is no earthquake. This type of movement, called creep, is so slow that it cannot be seen.

Try this: The San Andreas fault in California is always experiencing creep, or slow movement. Because of this, the land underneath Los Angeles is always moving north at a rate of about 2 inches per year. How far will Los Angeles move in 5 years? In 20 years? In 150 years?

Extra: How far has the ground underneath Los Angeles moved in the past 1,000 years? In the last 5,000 years?

4- Thunder and Distance

Imagine seeing a flash of lightning in the sky. After a short time, you'll hear the rumble of thunder. Count the number of seconds between seeing the lightning and hearing the thunder. Each second that passes is equal to a distance of one mile.

Try this: If 10 seconds pass between the lightning and thunder, how far off was the lightning?

Extra: How far away was lightning if 15 seconds passed before thunder was heard? 20 seconds? 30 seconds?

5- World's Fastest Dog

The greyhound is often called the fastest dog on the planet. This breed of dog has reached speeds of more than 41 miles per hour. This is faster than many speed limits on roads in your town!

Try this: Pretend a greyhound runs as fast as it can for 3 hours. How far has it travelled in that amount of time?

Extra: Imagine you drove in a car at 60 miles per hour for 1 hour. Also imagine a greyhound ran at 41 miles per hour for 2 hours. Which would travel farther, the car or the dog?

6- Earth Speed

Earth travels in an orbit around the sun. The speed of the Earth as it orbits the sun is 66,641 miles per hour.

Try this: If Earth orbits the sun at 66,641 miles per hour, how far does Earth travel in 2 hours?

Extra: In a week (7 days), how far does Earth travel?

7- Falcon Flight

The peregrine falcon lives in almost every country around the world. This bird of prey has been known to fly at speeds as high as 217 miles per hour.

Try this: How far would the fastest peregrine falcon fly in 3 hours?

Extra: How far would the fastest peregrine falcon fly in 9 hours?

8- Fast Cars

In 1983, Richard Noble took a drive in his jet-powered car, the *Thrust 2*. Richard reached a speed of just over 633 miles per hour.

Try this: If Richard drove the *Thrust 2* for 5 hours, how far would he travel?

Extra: How far would he travel if he drove the *Thrust 2* for 8 hours?

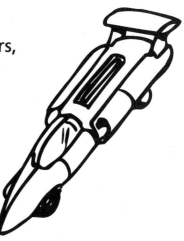

9- Speedy Spider

Some spiders in Africa are so fast that they can catch and eat small geckos and other lizards. These spiders have been seen travelling at 10 miles per hour.

Try this: How far could one of these speedy spiders travel in 3 hours?

Extra: How far could one of these spiders travel in 7 hours?

10- French Friends

Gustave Eiffel designed the famous Eiffel Tower in Paris, France. He was also the engineer for the Statue of Liberty located in New York City. The Statue of Liberty was first built in Paris. Then it was taken apart and shipped to New York.

Try this: The French ship *Isere* sailed to New York with 254 crates containing the pieces of the statue. If it took 3 people to unload each crate, how many people were needed to unload the ship?

Extra: If it took 9 people to unload each crate, how many people would be needed?

11- Miles per Gallon

Cars, planes, buses, and trucks are types of vehicles that use gasoline for fuel. It is important to know how much gasoline a vehicle uses. What if a pilot didn't know how far her plane could fly on a tank of gas? Or if you bought a car that used more gasoline than a big truck?

Try this: A typical car has a gas tank that holds 20 gallons of gasoline. If that car can travel 19 miles on a gallon, how far can it go on a full tank?

Extra: If the car mentioned above is driven from San Francisco to Phoenix and uses up 2 tanks of gas, how far is it between the cities?

12- Movie Multiplication

Movies consist of many separate images called frames, lined up in a row. Each frame is slightly different. For example, one frame could show a soccer ball. The next frame might show a foot kicking the ball. When these frames are played together, we see the motion of the ball being kicked.

Try this: Twenty-four frames are needed to make a second of film. This is called "24 frames per second." How many frames does it take to make one minute of film?

Extra: An average movie is 90 minutes. How many frames are necessary to make an average movie?

13- Rocket Science

In 1969, the three astronauts of *Apollo 11* travelled 240,000 miles to reach Earth's moon. However, the first liquid-fueled rocket flight occurred much earlier in history. In 1929, Robert Goddard launched the first of these type of rockets.

Try this: Goddard's first rocket flight lasted for 2.5 seconds and reached a height of 41 feet. What is the total distance this rocket had travelled after it returned to the ground?

Extra: What is the total round-trip distance the crew of *Apollo 11* travelled on their flight to the moon and back?

14- Terrific Trains

Throughout history, trains have used many different types of fuels, including coal, wood, diesel fuel, and electricity. The world's first public electric railroad opened in Germany in 1881. To run this train, 1.5 miles of track were used.

Try this: A train track consists of two sets of rails, one set for the left wheels and one for the right. If the first public electric train track was 1.5 miles long, what was the total amount of rail used?

Extra: The Canadian Pacific Railroad's transcontinental route was completed in 1886. The length of this railroad is 2,880 miles. How much rail was used for this railroad?

15- Big Bikes

Old-fashioned bicycles had very large front wheels. When these bikes were popular, inventors had a good reason for the big front wheels. They thought that the bigger wheels made the bike travel farther. One rotation of a wheel that was 60 inches tall went farther than one that was 10 inches tall.

Try this: A big-wheeled bike has a 60-inch wheel, and a single rotation of this wheel allows the bike to travel 15 feet. How far will this bike travel with 10 rotations?

Extra: How far can this same bike travel with 109 rotations?

16- Mountain Math

Mount Everest is the highest mountain in the world. This 29,028-foot tall mountain is located in the Himalayas between Tibet and Nepal.

Try this: One person, Ang Rita Sherpa, has climbed Mount Everest 8 times. What is the total distance he climbed in all 8 climbs?

Extra: In 1992, 32 men and 8 women reached the top of Everest in one day. What is the total distance all 40 of these people climbed?

17- Sun Power

Most cars need gasoline to run. However, a few cars use the energy of the sun to run. These are called *solar-powered* cars. Solar-powered cars have special batteries that convert the energy of the sun into electricity.

Try this: Molly Brennan drove a solar-powered car that reached a speed of 48 miles per hour. At this speed, how far would Molly travel in 11 hours?

Extra: How far would Molly travel in 24 hours?

18- Floating on Air

Hovercraft vehicles travel across land or water by floating on a cushion of air. Downward pointing jets provide the air cushion that lifts the vehicle.

Try this: One of the fastest hovercraft was able to travel on water at a speed of 105 miles per hour. How far could this vehicle travel in 11 hours?

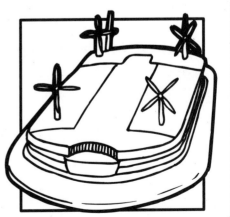

Extra: How far could this hovercraft travel in 24 hours?

19- Fastest Planet

The planet Mercury has been recorded as the fastest orbiting planet. Mercury travels around the sun at an average speed of 107,030 miles per hour.

Try this: How far does Mercury travel in 3 hours?

Extra: How far does this planet travel in a 24-hour day?

20- Biplane Beauty

A biplane is a type of airplane that has two sets of wings, one above the other. These kinds of planes were widely used when air flight was in its early stages of development.

Try this: An Italian biplane built in 1941 was able to reach a speed of 323 miles per hour. How far could this plane fly in 12 hours?

Extra: How far could this plane fly in 48 hours?

21- Cricket-Chirping Temperature Gage

Crickets chirp faster as the temperature rises. Did you know that you can calculate what the temperature is by counting cricket chirps? Take a moment to study the following formula:

T = (0.3 x N) + 40

In this equation, T equals the temperature you are going to calculate, in degrees Fahrenheit. N equals the number of cricket chirps counted in a minute.

Try this: Imagine you counted 60 cricket chirps in a minute. What is the temperature? Hint: Multiply the number of cricket chirps by 0.3, then add 40 to this answer.

Extra: What is the temperature when there are 170 chirps per minute?

22- Los Angeles Travel Time

In Los Angeles, there are two kinds of roadways: high-speed freeways designed for longer journeys, and surface streets, meant for local traffic.

Try this: How far will you travel on the freeway if you drive for 1.5 hours at 50 miles per hour?

Extra: How far will you travel on the freeway if you drive for 1.5 hours at 65 miles per hour?

23- Library Fine

One of Benjamin Franklin's most important ideas was the free library. Before him, people had to pay money to check out books. Now, most libraries let you borrow books for free. But if you keep a book beyond its due day, you may have to pay a fine.

Try this: Imagine that a library fine is 3 cents a day. How much would the fine be after 13 days?

Extra: If a library fine is 8 cents a day, how much would you pay in one year (365 days)?

24- Radio Talk

The average rate of speech is 125 words a minute. Some fast-talking radio announcers speak 250 words per minute. The world record is 310 words per minute.

Try this: Imagine a radio annnoucer speaking 250 words per minute. How many words would she speak in 35 minutes?

Extra: How many words would the world record holder speak in 60 minutes?

25- The Terrific Tin Lizzie

Henry Ford made motor cars. He designed an assembly line to carry car parts to workers. The assembly line made a car ordinary people could afford. Henry Ford's Model T car was first sold in 1908. Nicknamed the *Tin Lizzie*, it could reach a top speed of 45 mph.

Try this: If you were travelling at top speed in a *Tin Lizzie*, how far would you travel in 7.5 hours?

Extra: At top speed in a *Tin Lizzie*, how far could you travel in 11.5 hours?

26- Wagon Train Travels

Around 1840, covered wagons took families across the United States. The wagons were pulled by teams of mules or oxen. The wagons traveled about 20 miles a day. The trip across country could take more than five months.

Try this: How far could the wagons travel in 3.5 days?

Extra: If the wagons traveled 20 miles a day, how far could the wagons travel in the month of October?

27- Super Stalagmites

A stalagmite is a rock formation that grows upward from a cave floor. Stalagmites grow from the ground up when drops of water containing dissolved limestone drip to the cave's floor. Stalagmites can grow to be more than 45 feet tall and 30 feet wide.

Try this: If a cave floor had 9 stalagmites that were each 45 feet tall, how tall would they be if you put one on top of the other?

Extra: If a cave had 16 stalagmites that were each 30 feet wide, how much of the cave floor would they cover?

28- One, Two, Three

Bicycles were invented more than 200 years ago. Tricycles have three wheels, bicycles have two, and unicycles have one.

Try this: How many wheels would 150 bicycles have all together?

Extra: How many wheels would 150 tricycles have all together?

29- Kangaroo-Mobile

Some animals travel faster than people. A kangaroo can travel up to 40 miles per hour. In 1865, British law limited self-propelled road vehicles to 4 mph. This means that a kangaroo could travel 10 times faster than someone in a car.

Try this: In 1865, how far would a car travel in 10.5 hours?

Extra: How far would a kangaroo travel in 10.5 hours?

30- Studying Stalactites

A stalactite is a rock formation that hangs from the ceiling of a cave. Stalactites grow slowly. The fastest ones might grow 12 inches in 100 years. However, most stalactites grow only about .5 inch in 100 years!

Try this: How large could one of the fastest stalactites grow in 150 years?

Extra: How big could an average stalactite grow in 700 years?

31- Go, Go Gorillas!

Gorillas live only in deep rain forests in central Africa. The male gorilla has a silver back, can be 6.5 feet tall, and can weigh more than 600 pounds! Although male gorillas look fairly ferocious, they only fight if they have to protect their families.

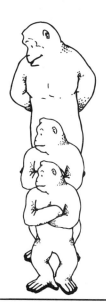

Try this: How tall would 7 gorillas be if you stacked one on top of the other?

Extra: How much would 7 gorillas weigh?

32- Big Bugs!

The atlas moth is one of the largest moths. It has a wingspan of 10-12 inches. The tiger centipede, an orange-and-black-striped centipede, can grow to be over 9 inches long. A curly haired tarantula can grow to be 3.5 inches across.

Try this: If you found 93 centipedes lined end to end, how long would they reach?

Bonus: If you lined up 23 tarantulas, how long would they be across?

33- Harley-Davidson

The *Sportster* is a type of motorcycle built by Harley-Davidson. The peanut-shaped gas tank on the *Sportster* is designed to give the bike a slim, sleek look.

Try this: A rider can drive a *Sporster* about 90 miles on one full tank of gas. How far will this rider go on 1/4 tank of gasoline?

Extra: How far will this rider go on 5/8 of a tank of gasoline?

34- Incredible Iguanas

Iguanas vary in size from 14 inches to 6 feet. Iguanas live in rain forests, on islands, and in deserts. They mostly eat fruits, vegetables, and leaves. Some iguanas also eat insects and small rodents. An iguana's tail can be longer than its body!

Try this: If an iguana's body was 14 inches long, and its tail was 1.75 times as long as its body, how long would its tail be?

Extra: If an iguana's body was 3 feet long, and its tail was .75 as long as its body, how long would the iguana be all together?

35- Big Money

The biggest coins ever minted were created in Sweden. The huge rectangular coins were called platmynt or plate money. The largest, the ten-Daler plate, weighed 42 lb.

Try this: If you had 12 ten-Daler plates, how much would they weigh?

Extra: If you had 150 ten-Daler plates, how much would they weigh?

36- Mother of Exiles

The inscription on the Statue of Liberty refers to the "mighty woman with a torch" as the *Mother of Exiles*. The seven spikes of her crown are said to represent the seven oceans of the world.

Try this: There are 354 steps from the statue's base to her crown. If you walked up 1/3 of the steps, how many steps did you walk?

Extra: How many steps would you make if you walked 2/8 of the steps?

37- Smith River Math

The Smith River is located near the border between California and Oregon. Steelhead trout swim from the ocean into the river and lay their eggs upstream.

Try this: Imagine 5 people going fishing, and the group catches 15 fish. They decide to divide the fish evenly among themselves. If each person gets 1/5, how many fish does each person bring home?

Extra: If the group catches 30 fish, and they release 2/3 of these fish, how many would they have left?

38- Mother Camels

Camels that live in China have two humps. They are called Bactrian. Female camels nurse their young for 14-16 months. One type of camel, called the Alxa, can produce more than 3 lb of milk a day. The Sonid camel can produce up to 7 lb of milk a day.

Try this: If an Alxa camel was milked for a year, how many pounds of milk could it produce?

Extra: If a Sonid camel was milked for a year, how much milk could it produce?

39- Carrying Camels

Bactrian camels live in the Gobi steppe of Central Asia. They can withstand extremely hot and cold temperatures. There are 15 million domestic Bactrians, but only 600 to 900 live in the wild. Bactrians can travel many miles while carrying loads of over 500 pounds.

Try this: If 900 Bactrian camels could each carry a load of 500 pounds, how many pounds could they carry in all?

Extra: If the 15 million domestic Bactrian camels could each carry 500 pounds, how many pounds could they carry in all?

40- Egyptian Displays

New galleries at the British Museum are dedicated to ancient Egyptian archaeology. It spans Egyptian history from the age of the pyramids to the Roman invasion.

Try this: If there are 17 artifacts on display in each gallery, and there are 63 galleries, how many artifacts are displayed?

Extra: If 13 visitors can fit in each gallery, how many people can look at the display at once?

41- Dining Elephants

Elephants live in woodlands, grasslands, and forests in Africa and parts of Asia. They can live to be 70 years old and can stand 6 to 12 feet at the shoulder. They eat an average of 400 to 600 pounds of food a day, of which 4/10ths is digested.

Try this: If an elephant ate 400 pounds of food in a day, how many pounds would it digest?

Extra: If 3 elephants each ate 600 pounds of food in a day, how many pounds would they digest in total?

42- Weighing Elephants

Elephants can weigh 5,000 to 14,000 pounds. They usually travel in herds made up of females and their calves. Herds can range in size from 20 to 200.

Try this: In a herd of 20 elephants, if each elephant weighed 5,000 pounds, how much would the entire herd weigh?

Extra: In a herd of 200 elephants, if each elephant weighed 14,000 pounds, how much would the entire herd weigh?

43- Home Demolition

In 1981, a man in Straffordshire, England, shut the front door of his 120-year-old house. He watched as 3/4 of the two-story house collapsed around him in a pile of dust and rubble.

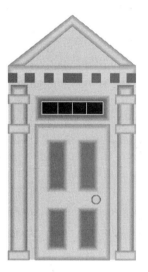

Try this: How much of the house would have been demolished if it had been 40 feet tall?

Extra: How much of the house would have been left standing if it had been 80 feet tall?

44- Don't Mess with the IRS

A man in Washington State underpaid his federal income taxes by one penny. He was fined $159.78.

Try this: If the fine was $159.78 per penny, how much would he have been fined if he had underpaid his taxes by 2 pennies?

Extra: How much would he have been fined if he had underpaid his federal income taxes by one dollar?

45- Viewing Niagara Falls

Niagara Falls is located on the border between Canada and the United States. Viewers watch the falls from an observation deck. They can also ride by the falls in a boat. About 20,000 bathtubs of water pour over the falls every second.

Try this: How many bathtubs full of water pour over the falls in one minute?

Extra: How many bathtubs full of water pour over the falls in one hour?

46- Marvelous Monet

Claude Monet was a famous French Impressionist painter. He painted a picture called *Fishing Boats Leaving the Harbor, Le Havre* in 1874.

Try this: If a harbor could hold 300 boats, and 2/3 of them were at sea, how many boats are at sea?

Extra: If a harbor could hold 300 boats, and 1/2 of them were at sea, how many boats are at sea?

47- Look Out, Ants!

One type of anteater can flick its tongue 160 times a minute. It is able to eat up to 30,000 ants each day!

Try this: How many times can an anteater flick its tongue in an hour?

Extra: How many times can an anteater flick its tongue in a day?

48- The Leaning Tower

Even before it was finished being built, the Leaning Tower of Pisa began sinking into the soft ground. It leans to one side, and each year it leans 1/20 of an inch more.

Try this: How far will it lean in the next 3 years?

Extra: How far will the tower lean in the next decade?

1- What's in a Whale?

A wide variety of whales swim in the world's oceans. The largest whale is the blue whale. The average blue whale grows to be 30 feet long.

Try this: If the average compact car is 6 feet long, how many cars would fit in a whale?

Extra: How many of your classmates would fit end to end in a whale?

2- Wise Water Watching

Water use at home is something we should all pay careful attention to. Our water supply is a valuable resource that must be used wisely.

Try this: A family of 5 uses about 840 gallons of water each day. How much water does a single person in this household use in a day?

Extra: If the amount of water a family uses in a day is cut in half, how much water does one person use?

3- John T. Scopes

John Scopes was a teacher in Dayton, Tennessee. He broke a state law forbidding the teaching of a certain subject. This subject was called evolution, which is the belief that human ancestors were from the ape family.

Try this: In 1925, John Scopes was fined $100 for breaking the law. If he paid the fine in 5 equal payments, how much was each payment?

Extra: If John's fine were $250, how much would each payment be?

4- Women in Space

The first woman in space was a citizen of the former Soviet Union. In 1963, Valentina Tereshkova orbited the Earth in the spaceship *Vostok 6*.

Try this: Valentina orbited around the Earth 48 times in 3 days. How many times did she orbit the Earth each day?

Extra: If Valentina could have made 51 orbits in 3 days, how many orbits would she have made each day?

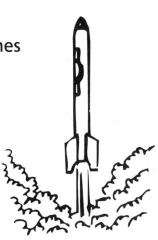

5- Hairy Math

The average person, male or female, loses about 525 hairs each week. These are replaced by new hairs, unless the person is going bald.

Try this: How many hairs does a person lose each day of a 7-day week?

Extra: If a person loses 770 hairs a week, how many does this person lose each day?

6- Typewriter Talent

The term *words per minute* is used to describe the number of words a person can type in one minute. A person who types 40 to 60 words per minute is considered a good typist.

Try this: Carol Waldschlager set a record for typing when she typed 880 words in 5 minutes. How many words per minute did she type?

Extra: Gregory Arakelian was able to type 474 words in 3 minutes. How many words per minute did he type?

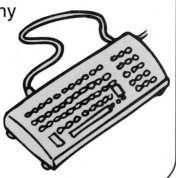

7- Big Burrito

A burrito is a kind of Mexican food. A round, thin piece of bread, called a tortilla, is wrapped around beans or meat, cheese, and vegetables.

Try this: A restaurant made a very large burrito in 1997. This burrito weighed about 4,460 pounds. If 10 people had to eat the whole burrito, how many pounds would each person eat?

Extra: How much burrito would 5 people have to eat?

8- Hamburger Heaven

The largest recorded hamburger ever made was 5,520 pounds. It was made as part of a county fair in 1989.

Try this: If 3 people had to eat all the hamburger, without ketchup, how many pounds would each person eat?

Extra: If you could eat 6 pounds of hamburger in a day, how many days would it take you to eat this 5,520-pound burger?

9- Michael Math

Concerts are music events where musicians play their songs in front of a live audience. Michael Jackson played his music for 7 nights in London, England.

Try this: Michael performed in front of a total of 504,000 people over 7 nights. How many people did he play for each night?

Extra: How many people per night would he have played for if he performed for 9 nights?

10- Theater Thinking

Some people like watching movies in theaters. Others prefer to see live theater events, such as plays and musicals. Dr. H. Howard Hughes of Texas has seen more than 6,000 shows.

Try this: Dr. Hughes saw these shows during the years 1957 to 1987. During these 30 years, how many shows did he see per year?

Extra: How many shows per year would he have seen if he attended a total of 9,000 shows?

11- Life in a Rain Forest

Many different mammals, birds, reptiles, and amphibians live in rain forests, from tiny mites to large jaguars. Rain falls nearly every day in tropical rain forests. There is usually at least 60 inches of rain per year.

Try this: How much rain could you expect to fall on an average day?

Extra: Imagine that it rained 72 inches in a year. How much rain could you expect to fall on an average day?

12- Towering Tree Tops

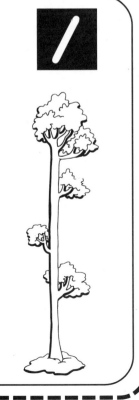

Trees in the rain forest have shallow roots. That's because the soil isn't rich. The roots take in the nutrients near the surface. Rain forest trees can be 200 feet tall. These trees tower over the top of the rain forest, which is called the canopy.

Try this: If you wanted to climb to the top of a rain forest tree, and you could climb 40 feet per hour, how many hours would it take until you reached the top?

Extra: Going down a tree can be slower than going up. If you could climb down at 12.5 feet per hour, how many hours would it take you to get to the bottom?

13- Gorgeous Gemstones

Gemstones include opals, diamonds, emeralds, rubies, and sapphires. The Hope Diamond has a bad reputation. People believe that it brings bad luck. It is 45.52 carats and is now in the Smithsonian Institution in Washington, D.C.

Try this: Imagine that a jeweler were going to cut the Hope Diamond into 10 different pieces. If each piece was equal, how many carats would each one be?

Extra: If a jeweler wanted to divide the Hope Diamond into 100 different equal pieces, how many carats would each be?

14- Playing with Piñatas

Piñatas are hollow figurines filled with goodies. The piñatas are hit with a stick until they break open. When they're broken, the goodies come out.

Try this: If it takes 18 hits before a piñata breaks, and each child gets to hit it 3 times, how many children will be able to have a turn?

Extra: If it takes 23 hits before a piñata breaks, and each child gets to hit it 3 times, how many children will have a turn? Round up to the nearest child.

15- Busy Bees

More than 50,000 bees can live in a hive. A bee can use its stinger only one time. The queen bee spends her life laying eggs.

Try this: If half of the bees in a hive of 50,000 wanted to start their own hive, how many would be left?

Extra: If one quarter of the bees in a hive of 50,000 moved to their own hive, how many would leave?

16- Cool Constellations

A constellation is a group of stars that resembles an imaginary object. The Big Dipper, part of a constellation, looks like a dipper or a ladle. Orion is a constellation that resembles a hunter. There are 88 constellations.

Try this: If you could view 8 constellations a night, how many nights would it take before you could see them all?

Extra: If you could view 3 constellations a night, how many nights would it take before you could see them all?

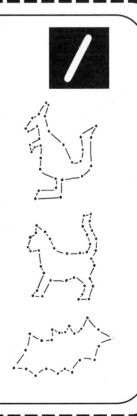

17- Hop on the Hubble

The Hubble Space Telescope (HST) is a satellite the size of a bus. It orbits the Earth every 97 minutes, traveling at 17,500 mph.

Try this: How many times can the Hubble Space Telescope orbit the Earth in 388 minutes?

Extra: One Earth day equals 1,440 minutes. How many times could the Hubble Space Telescope orbit the Earth in one day?

18- Traveling by Starlight

The stars were the first maps for ancient travelers. Arabs crossing sand dunes used the stars to find their way. So did sailors far from land. By studying the constellations and the brightest stars, Polynesians sailed from Tahiti to Hawaii. That's more than 3,000 miles!

Try this: If Polynesian sailors could travel 35 miles a day, how many days would it take them to get from Tahiti to Hawaii?

Extra: If Polynesian sailors could travel 30.5 miles a day, how many days would it take them to get from Tahiti to Hawaii?

19- Hello to Halley's Comet

Comets look like a blur of stars with a tail. These tails are millions of miles long. Ancient Greeks called them "long-haired stars." Comets look slow because they are so far away. The most famous comet is Halley's comet. It returns every 76 years. The next time will be in 2061.

Try this: If Halley's Comet appears every 76 years, how many times will it appear during a 304-year period?

Extra: How many times will it appear during a 1,000 year period? Round your answer to the nearest whole number.

20- Word Count

Approximately 250 typed words fit on an average sized sheet of paper, if the sentences are double spaced.

Try this: Imagine you have written a story about exploring that is 4,000 words long. How many typed, double-spaced pages long is it?

Extra: Imagine you added more to your exploring story and it is now 6,375 words long. How many pages is it?

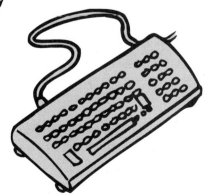

21- Sneaky Snakes

Snakes are a type of reptile that have no feet or legs. They travel along the ground by slithering. Some snakes are small, others are quite long. The longest snake is the python. It can grow to be 30 feet long.

Try this: If a football field is 300 feet long, how many pythons would fit across it end to end?

Extra: How many desks in your classroom lined end to end would equal the length of a python?

22- Metric Tessellation

A tessellation is a picture or design made by assembling small square tiles.

Try this: Suppose you are making a tesselated mural and you have to cover an area that is 2.8 square meters. Each tile you have covers a .02 square meter area. How many tiles will you need to cover the entire area?

Extra: How many tiles would you need to cover a 15 square meter area?

23- The Unsinkable Ship

The *Titanic* was called "unsinkable." On its first voyage, the *Titanic* hit an iceberg and sank: 1,513 people died. A total of 2,200 people were aboard. Many of the people died because of a shortage of lifeboats.

Try this: If each lifeboat held 25 people, how many lifeboats would have been required to save every person on the *Titanic*?

Extra: If each lifeboat held 23 people, how many lifeboats would have been required? (Round up to the nearest whole number.)

24- Hop on a Hovercraft

A hovercraft rides on a cushion of high-pressure air that reduces the friction between the craft and the surface over which it travels. Modern hovercrafts can carry 220 tons of cargo for 560 miles.

Try this: If you had 1,100 tons of cargo, how many hovercrafts would you need to carry it?

Extra: If you had 11,000 tons of cargo, how many hovercrafts would you need?

25- Slow Sloths

Sloths are slow-moving animals. They actually provide homes to different animals. Beetles, mites, and moths can live in a sloth's fur. One sloth was found with 978 beetles living on it!

Try this: If half the beetles left the sloth and moved to another sloth, how many beetles would be left?

Extra: If the 978 beetles lived on 4 different sloths, how many beetles would live on each sloth?

26- The Great Wall of China

The Great Wall is called the Long Wall of Ten Thousand Li in China. This remarkable structure was designed to follow natural land formations. It was built for protection against foreign invaders. The wall stretches 1,500 miles to the eastern coast of China.

Try this: If you could walk 15 miles a day, how many days would it take you to walk from one end of the Great Wall to the other?

Extra: If you could run 20.7 miles a day, how many days would it take you to make the journey from one end of the Great Wall to the other?

27- Feeding a Baby

Tiny babies have to eat often, as much as 8 times a day. A 9.5 pound baby should eat approximately 28.86 ounces a day.

Try this: If a parent fed the baby 6 times a day, how many ounces would the baby need at each feeding?

Extra: How many ounces per feeding would the baby need for 8 daily feedings?

28- Terrific Turtles

There are between 250 and 300 types of turtles. Turtles that live on land are usually called tortoises. Turtles that live in the water are usually called terrapins. The largest turtle was a leatherback. It weighed 2,016 pounds!

Try this: If an average pet turtle weighed 4 pounds, how many pet turtles would it take to be as he. the largest turtle?

Extra: If an average sea turtle weighed 215.7 pounds, how many sea turtles would it take to be as heavy as the largest turtle?

29- Learning Languages

Sir William Rowan Hamilton was an Irish mathematician who lived from 1805 to 1865. He was a child prodigy who learned 13 different languages by the time he was 13 years old.

Try this: If Sir William Rowan Hamilton started learning languages when he was 5, how many would he have to learn each year?

Extra: If Sir William Rowan Hamilton started learning languages at age 7.5, how many would he have to learn each year?

30- Visiting the Panthéon

The Panthéon is a building located in the Latin Quarter in Paris. It is 360 feet wide and 272 feet high. Its crypt contains the tombs of Voltaire and Rousseau.

Try this: If you could put one bench in every 6 feet of the building, how many benches would fit inside?

Extra: If you could fit one tourist in every 1.5 feet, how many people could fit?

31- The Amazing Eiffel

Paris's Eiffel Tower was the star attraction of the Universal Exhibition of 1889. The tower is made of a framework of girders. It reaches a height of 984 feet.

Try this: If you were to climb the Eiffel Tower at a rate of 90 feet an hour, how many hours would it take you?

Extra: If you could scale the Eiffel Tower at a rate of 101.5 feet an hour, how many hours would it take you?

32- Putting Together a Piñata

Hitting a piñata is a fun party activity. Making one can be even more fun. Piñatas are started by inflating a balloon and covering the balloon with strips of newspaper dipped into a flour and water paste.

Try this: If it takes 200 strips of newspaper to cover a balloon, and you can put on 10 strips a minute, how long will it take to cover the balloon?

Extra: If it takes 225 strips of newspaper to cover a balloon, and you can put on 10 strips a minute, how long will it take to completely cover the balloon?

33- London Celebrations

In London, on special days, gun salutes are fired at 12 noon in Hyde Park and at 1 p.m. from the Tower of London. Two special days are the Queen's real birthday, which is April 21, and the Queen's official birthday, which is June 12.

Try this: If it took 10 minutes to get from Hyde Park to the Tower of London, how many times could you go back and forth between the two gun salutes?

Extra: If it took 20 minutes, how many trips could you make?

34- The Wright Flyer

On December 17, 1903, Orville Wright piloted the *Flyer*. The plane flew for 12 seconds and a distance of 37 feet. The longest flight that day was 852 feet and lasted 59 seconds.

Try this: How many feet per second did the *Flyer* travel on its first flight?

Extra: How many feet per second did the *Flyer* travel on its longest flight on December 17?

35- Long Overdue

The longest overdue book on record in the United States was borrowed in 1823 from the University of Cincinnati Medical Library. It was returned in 1968 by the great-grandson of the borrower. If he had been asked to pay the fine, it would have equaled $2,264.

Try this: How much was the fine per year?

Extra: If half of the fine was paid, how much would it be per year?

36- Ellis Island

Between 1892 and 1954, 12 million immigrants were processed at Ellis Island. Today, more than 4/10, or over 100 million, of all living Americans can trace their roots to an ancestor who came through Ellis Island.

Try this: Over the 62 years that Ellis Island processed immigrants, how many on average were processed each year?

Extra: If your town had a population of 50,000, and 4/10 had ancestors who came through Ellis Island, how many would that be?

37- Quick Versus Slow

Some animals can travel as fast as a car, while others move at a slow and steady pace. A cheetah can run at 70 miles per hour. A lion can run at 50 miles per hour. A snail can move at .03 mile per hour.

Try this: How many hours would it take a snail to travel one mile?

Extra: How many hours would it take a cheetah to travel 35 miles?

38- Cock-a-Doodle Dollars

During a National Rooster Crow competition, one rooster crowed 82 times in 30 minutes. He won his owner 150 silver dollars.

Try this: How many times did the rooster crow per minute?

Extra: How many silver dollars did the rooster earn per minute?

39- Baseball Pitch

Some baseball pitchers can throw a fastball at 95 miles per hour.

Try this: How long does it take a 60-mile-per-hour fastball to travel from the pitching mound to the plate (approximately 60 feet)? Keep in mind 1 mile equals 5,280 feet.

Extra: How long would it take for a 95-mile-per-hour fastball to travel to the plate?

40- Generations

A generation is the average period between the birth of parents and their children. Most experts use 30 years as the measure of a generation.

Try this: How many generations have there been in the past 100 years?

Extra: How many generations have there been during the 2,000 years of the current Western calendar?

41- Moon Bicycle Trip

The distance from the Earth to the moon changes during the year. But the average distance is 240,000 miles.

Try this: If it were possible to bicycle to the moon, how long would it take if the bicyclist could ride at 15 miles per hour?

Extra: How long would it take if the bicyclist could ride at 25 miles per hour?

42- Moon Gravity

The gravity on the moon is about 1/6 the gravity on the Earth. This means that a 6-pound weight on the Earth would weigh 1 pound on the moon.

Try this: How much would a 200-pound person weigh on the moon?

Extra: How much would you weigh on the moon?

1- Parking Lot Perimeter

The perimeter of an object can be found by adding up the lengths of all the object's sides. For example, a square has 4 equal length sides. If each side is 2 feet long, then the square's perimeter is
2 + 2 + 2 + 2 = 8 feet long.

Try this: Imagine a parking lot that is shaped like a rectangle. Two of the sides are 50 feet long and 2 are 25 feet long. What is the perimeter of the parking lot?

Extra: What is the perimeter of a parking lot that has 2 sides 100 feet long and 2 sides 50 feet long?

2- Pentagon Perimeter

A pentagon is a 5-sided figure. There is also a building that is called the Pentagon. This building has 5 sides.

Try this: The perimeter of a pentagon is the sum of the lengths of all its 5 sides. Imagine a pentagon with sides that are each 2 feet long. What is this pentagon's perimeter?

Extra: What is the perimeter of a pentagon that has sides that are each 25 feet long?

3- Triangle Perimeter

A triangle is a 3-sided figure. There is a special type of triangle called an isosceles (pronounced *i saw sa leez*) triangle. *Iso* means equal. An isosceles triangle has 3 sides of equal length.

Try this: The perimeter of a triangle is measured by adding the lengths of its 3 sides. Imagine an isosceles triangle that has 3 sides that are each 6 feet long. What is this triangle's perimeter?

Extra: Imagine an isosceles triangle with sides of 25 feet. What is this triangle's perimeter?

4- Hexagon Perimeter

Poly is a Greek word that means *many*. A polygon is a figure with many sides. A hexagon is a type of polygon with 6 sides.

Try this: The perimeter of a polygon is measured by adding the lengths of all its sides. Imagine a hexagon that has 6 sides that are each 5 feet long. What is the perimeter of this hexagon?

Extra: Imagine a hexagon with 25-foot-long sides. What is this hexagon's perimeter?

5- Heptagon Perimeter

Poly is a Greek word that means *many*. A polygon is a figure with many sides. A heptagon is special type of polygon with 7 sides.

Try this: The perimeter of a polygon is measured by adding the lengths of all its sides. Imagine a heptagon that has 7 sides that are 10 feet long each. What is the perimeter of this heptagon?

Extra: Imagine a heptagon with sides 35 feet long. What is this heptagon's perimeter?

6- Octagon Perimeter

Poly is a Greek word that means *many*. A polygon is a figure with many sides. An octagon is special type of polygon with 8 sides.

Try this: The perimeter of a polygon is measured by adding the lengths of all its sides. Imagine an octagon that has 8 sides that are each 15 feet long. What is the perimeter of this octagon?

Extra: Imagine an octagon with sides 40 feet long. What is this octagon's perimeter?

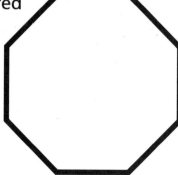

MATH START-UPS © 2000 MONDAY MORNING BOOKS, INC.

7- Nonagon Perimeter

Poly is a Greek word that means *many*. A polygon is a figure with many sides. A nonagon is special type of polygon with 9 sides.

Try this: The perimeter of a polygon is measured by adding the lengths of all its sides. Imagine a nonagon that has 9 sides that are each 17 feet long. What is the perimeter of this nonagon?

Extra: Imagine a nonagon with 15-foot-long sides. What is this nonagon's perimeter?

8- Decagon Perimeter

Poly is a Greek word that means *many*. A polygon is a figure with many sides. A decagon is special type of polygon with 10 sides.

Try this: The perimeter of a polygon is measured by adding the lengths of all its sides. Imagine a decagon that has 10 sides that are each 6 feet long. What is the perimeter of this decagon?

Extra: Imagine a decagon with sides 12 feet long. What is this decagon's perimeter?

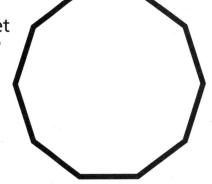

9- Square Area

Squares are four-sided polygons that have sides of equal length. The area of a square is measured by multiplying the length of one side by the length of another side.

Try this: Imagine that you are looking out of window that is shaped like a square. The length of each side of the window is 2 feet. What is the area of the window?

Extra: Imagine the window you are looking out of has sides that are 8 feet long. What is the area of this window?

10- Rectangle Area

A rectangle is a four-sided polygon. Two longer sides of the rectangle are called the *length*, and the two shorter sides are called the *width*. The area of a rectangle is measured by multiplying one of the length sides by one of the width sides.

Try this: A parking lot is shaped like a rectangle. The length of this parking lot is 45 feet and the width is 20 feet. What is the area of this parking lot?

Extra: An airport landing strip is shaped like a rectangle. The length of this strip is 1,000 feet and its width is 75 feet. What is the area of this landing strip?

Resources

Student Activity Log

Name: _____

Card Number	Card Type (Addition, Subtraction, Multiplication, Division, Geometry)	Answer	Checked Answer (From Teacher)

MATH START-UPS © 2000 MONDAY MORNING BOOKS, INC.

Number Whiz Play

Characters
Student 1
Student 2
Student 3
Number Whiz

Student 1: What answer did you get for the third problem?

Student 2: I got 90 seconds.

Student 3: I got 195 words.

Student 1: I got 2,650 dollars.

Student 2: You're wrong. I'm right.

Student 3: I'm right. You're wrong.

Student 1: You're both wrong. I'm right.

(Sound: A drum roll or a fanfare signals the entrance of Number Whiz, a character wearing a shirt with the words "Number Whiz" on it.)

Student 2: Look. It's Number Whiz, the smartest problem solver in the world.

Student 3: Number Whiz, can you help us?

Number Whiz: You can *count* on me. What's the problem?

Student 1: The problem is math word problems.

Student 2: You have to be a genius to figure out this stuff.

Number Whiz Play

Number Whiz: I don't think so. Although I happen to be a genius myself, most people can solve math problems if they know how.

Student 3: Then tell us how.

Number Whiz: Do you have a problem to work on?

Student 1: We have plenty.

Student 2: For example, we were just trying this one: "A radio station charges 1100 dollars to broadcast a standard one-minute radio commercial on the weekend. The average announcer speaks at the rate of 130 words a minute. How much would the station charge for a commercial that is one and a half times longer than the standard commercial if the commercial plays on Sunday night?"

Number Whiz: OK, what's the first thing to do with this sort of problem?

Student 3: Guess at the answer.

Number Whiz: Nope.

Student 1: Turn on your calculator.

Number Whiz: Sorry.

Student 2: Start to cry.

Number Whiz: I don't think so.

All together: Well then, what do you do?

Number Whiz Play

Number Whiz: My advice is to first make sure you know what the question is. Look for the question mark.

Student 3: You mean, "How much money would the station charge for a 90-second commercial?"

Number Whiz: Exactly. Now, what does that tell you?

Student 1: That the answer is going to be a certain amount of money.

Student 2: (Sadly) So my answer of 90 seconds is wrong.

Number Whiz: Yes. But where did it come from?

Student 2: The words about a commercial that is one and a half times longer than the standard commercial. Since this commercial is one and a half times a minute, and since a minute is 60 seconds, I got 90 seconds.

Number Whiz: That makes sense, and you can use that fact in solving the problem. But always remember to keep in mind what you're looking for. In this case, it isn't time. It's money.

Student 2: I get it.

Student 3: So when I came up with 195 words, I made the same kind of mistake. I figured out how many words would be spoken in a minute and a half.

Number Whiz: Yes, and that might be useful if you had been asked to figure out the length of a commercial in words. But in this case, that information isn't needed.

Number Whiz Play

Student 3: Then why did the person who wrote the question include the fact about the number of words that can be read in a minute?

Number Whiz: In the real world, you often have to sift through information to find out what you need to solve a problem. This requires careful thinking. People who write word problems often include facts that aren't useful just to help you become better at solving problems.

Student 1: (claps hands) I got the right answer. Told you so. I did it. The problem asked for an amount of money, and that's what I said: 2650 dollars. I'm a genius.

Number Whiz: Can you explain how you got the answer?

Student 1: Why?

Number Whiz: By telling how you solved a problem, you reinforce your skills. You can also catch mistakes.

Student 1: OK. The problem tells what a one-minute commercial costs. That's 1100 dollars.

Number Whiz: But that's only for the weekends.

Student 1: Right. But the problem says the commercial will play on Sunday night, which is part of the weekend.

Number Whiz: That's an example of using general knowledge to solve a problem.

Student 1: I then multiplied one and a half times 1100 dollars to get the charge for a commercial that was one and a half times longer than a standard commercial.

Number Whiz Play

Number Whiz: Exactly how did you do the math?

Student 1: I set up the work like this: 1,100 is the multiplicand; 1.5 is the multiplier.

$$\begin{array}{r} \$1{,}100 \\ \times\ 1.5 \\ \hline 5500 \\ +1100 \\ \hline \$2{,}650.0 \end{array}$$

Five times 1,100 is 5,500; one time 1,100 is 1,100. Add them together, and you get $2,650. Right?

Number Whiz: Let's see. Suppose that the problem asked you what a two-minute commercial would have cost.

Student 1: That would have been easy. Two times 1,100 is 2,200.

Number Whiz: But in this case, the commercial isn't two times as long. It's only one and a half times as long.

Student 2: Then the answer should be less than 2,200.

Student 1: Uh oh. I wasn't right. Oh no.

Number Whiz: Don't get too upset. There's a real lesson to be learned here. You did a good job of figuring out the problem. You just forgot the final step.

Student 1: What's that?

Number Whiz Play

Number Whiz: To check your work. That means not only going over your math work. It also means asking yourself, "Does the answer make sense?" In this case, because you could easily figure out what a two-minute commercial would cost, you could see immediately that something was wrong with your answer.

Student 2: There's so much to think about.

Number Whiz: True, but that's good. These problems are like brain exercise. The more you do, the smarter you'll become.

Student 3: Can people really improve their brains?

Number Whiz: Absolutely. I think you'll find that the really smart people in the world are people who do a lot of thinking.

Student 1: I guess we're lucky then because we have a ton of problems to work on.

Number Whiz: Go to it. But before you do, let me sum up what we've learned about problem solving:
1. Never guess wildly.
2. Make sure you know what kind of answer you're looking for.
3. Determine which information is relevant. Find the question. In some cases, drawing a picture can help.
4. Decide on the math operation called for: adding, subtracting, multiplying, or dividing. Sometimes you'll do more than one.
5. Set up the work and do it carefully.
6. Check your math work.
7. Ask yourself if the answer makes sense.

Roman Numerals

1	I		19	XIX
2	II		20	XX
3	III		30	XXX
4	IV		40	XL
5	V		50	L
6	VI		60	LX
7	VII		70	LXX
8	VIII		80	LXXX
9	IX		90	XC
10	X		100	C
11	XI		200	CC
12	XII		300	CCC
13	XIII		400	CD
14	XIV		500	D
15	XV		600	DC
16	XVI		700	DCC
17	XVII		800	DCCC
18	XVIII		900	CM
			1,000	M

Number Prefixes

1	uni-, mon-, mono-
2	bi-, di-
3	tri-
4	quadr-, tetr-
5	pent-, penta-
6	hex-, hexa-
7	hepta-
8	oct-, octa-, octo-
9	nona-
10	dec-, deca-
100	cent-
1000	kilo-
million	mega-
billion	giga-

Conversions

U.S. Customary Units to Metric Units

Today, the chief systems for weights and measures are the English units of measurement and the metric system. The United States is one of the few countries still using the English units of measurements.

1 inch = 2.54 centimeters
1 inch = 0.0254 meter
1 foot = 30.48 centimeters
1 foot = .3048 meter
1 yard = 0.9144 meter
1 mile = 1.6093 kilometers
1 square inch = 6.4516 square centimeters
1 square foot = 0.0929 square meter
1 square yard = 0.8361 square meter
1 acre = 0.4047 hectare
1 cubic inch = 16.3871 cubic centimeters
1 cubic foot = 0.0283 cubic meter
1 cubic yard = 0.7646 cubic meter
1 quart (liquid) = 0.9464 liter
1 ounce = 28.3495 grams
1 pound = 0.4536 kilogram

Conversions

Metric Units to U.S. Customary Units

The metric system of weights and measures was planned in France and adopted there in 1799. Many countries use this system today. It is based on a unit of length called the meter and a unit of mass called the kilogram.

1 centimeter = 0.3937 inch
1 centimeter = 0.0328 foot
1 meter = 39.3701 inches
1 meter = 3.2808 feet
1 meter = 1.0936 yards
1 kilometer = 0.621 mile
1 square centimeter = 0.1550 square inch
1 square meter = 10.7639 square feet
1 square meter = 1.196 square yards
1 hectare = 2.471 acres
1 cubic centimeter = 0.061 cubic inch
1 cubic meter = 1.308 cubic yards
1 liter = 1.0567 quarts (liquid)
1 gram = 0.0353 ounce
1 kilogram = 2.2046 pounds

Answer Key

Addition

1. Adding Oysters: 20 + 20 + 20 + 20 + 20 + 20 = 120;
120 + 120 + 120 +120 + 120 + 120 + 120 + 120 + 120 + 120 + 120
+ 120 + 120 + 120 + 120 = 1,800

2. Georgia Peaches: 118 + 118 = 236; 236 + 118 + 118 = 472

3. Red Kangaroos: 42 + 42 = 84; 84 + 42 = 126

4. Moon Math: 18 + 2 + 0 = 20; 0 + 2 + 15 + 0 + 16 + 8 + 1 + 18 + 1 = 61

5. Great Pyramids: 481 + 218 = 699; 699 + 472 = 1,171

6. Whale of a Meal: 4,400 + 4,400 = 8,800; 8,800 + 8,800 = 17,600

7. Counting Cars: 600 + 750 = 1,350; 1,000 + 2,500 = 3,500

8. Snow Pack: 14 + 28 = 42; 32 + 22 = 54

9. Picture Perfect: 24 + 36 = 60; 36 + 36 = 72

10. Making Books: 24 + 28 = 52; 45 + 65 = 110

11. Alphabet Addition: varies by first name; 351

12. Mammal Math: 70 + 120 = 190; 90 + 120 = 210

13. Letter Values: 4 + 5 + 20 + 5 + 18 + 13 + 9 + 14 + 1 + 20 + 9
+ 15 + 14 = 147; 20 + 15 + 2 + 5 + 15 + 18 + 14 + 15 + 20 + 20 +
15 + 2 + 5 = 166

14. Book Value: 16.50 + 10.00 = 26.50; 26.50 + 9.95 = 36.45

15. Pizza Plus: 8.00 + 14.30 = 22.30; 8.00 + 1.50 + 1.50 = 11.00

16. The Play's the Thing: 48.00 + 62.50 = 110.50; 110.50 + 56.35 = 166.85

17. Toll Bridges: 3.00 + 1.50 = 4.50; 3.00 + 1.50 + 1.50 = 6.00

18. A Bevy of Bicycles: 4 + 4 = 8; 1 + 3 + 4 = 8

19. La Tomatina: 225 + 198 = 423; 423 + 387 = 810

20. Hungry Bats: 612 + 546 = 1,158; 5,654 + 4,817 = 10,471

21. Tallying the Rain Forest: 750 + 750 = 1,500; 1,500 + 125 + 400 + 100 + 60 = 2,185

22. Using Hieroglyphics: 3,100 + 400 = 3,500; 3,100 - 3054 = 46

Subtraction

1. Jet Plane Planning: 500 - 250 = 250; 3,600 - 2,512 = 1,088

2. Big Tooth: 55 - 26 = 29; 55 - 20 = 35

3. School Days: 365 - 180 = 185; 365 - 220 = 145

4. George Washington: 1789 - 1732 = 57; 1789 - 1731 = 58

5. Fishing for Math: 5,613 - 4,276 = 1,337; 9,010 - 8,238 = 772

MATH START-UPS © 2000 MONDAY MORNING BOOKS, INC.

Answer Key

6. Civil Engineering: 6,468 - 6,198 = 270; 9,234 - 8,496 = 738

7. How Far?: 2,835 - 310 = 2,525; 2,835 - 1,287 = 1,548

8. Border Math: 3,987 - 1,933 = 2,054; 3,987 + 1,933 = 5,920

9. Bug Out: 177 - 100 = 77; 1,000 - 375 = 625

10. Mayor Math: 1967 - 1927 = 40; 1971 - 1927 = 44

11. Tall Trees: 367.5 - 275 = 92.5; 102.6 - 10.4 = 92.2

12. Lizard Length: 10.16 - 0.06 = 10.10; 10.16 - .16 = 10.00

13. Big Birds: 6.5 - 0.18 = 6.32; 9 - 6.5 = 2.5

14. Pinniped Problem: 21.33 - 3.9 = 17.43; 21.33 - 4.79 = 16.54

15. Swimming the Channel: 7.67 - 7.28 = 0.39; 18.61 - 12.08 = 6.53

16. Oh Deer!: 7.67 - 1.25 = 6.42; 7.67 - 5.83 = 1.84

17. Noisy Monkey: 2.93 - 2.86 = 0.07; 2.93 - 0.55 = 2.38

18. Short and Tall: 6.12 - 3.08 = 3.04; 8.91 - 6.12 = 2.79

19. Deep in the Ocean: 4.8 - 3.28 = 1.52; 24 - 8.08 = 15.92

20. High Art: 82.5 - 11.8 = 70.7; 82.5 - 11.9 = 70.6

21. Floating Bridge: 12,596 - 7,518 = 5,078; 12,596 - 3,239 = 9,357

22. Moon Temperature: 243 - 58 = 185; 58 - (-261) = 319

23. Plant Lives: 21,000 - (-884) = 21,884; 29,028 - 21,000 = 8,028

24. General Hannibal: 247 - 217 = 30; 247 - 182 = 65

Multiplication

1. A Day on Mars: 24.7 x 7 = 172.9; 172.9 x 52 = 8,990.8

2. Bottom of the Sea: 100 x 6 = 600; 6,000 x 6 = 36,000

3. Fault-Line Forecasting: 2 x 5 = 10; 2 x 20 = 40; 2 x 150 = 300; 1,000 x 2 = 2,000; 5,000 x 2 = 10,000

4. Thunder and Distance: 10 x 1 = 10; 15 x 1 = 15; 20 x 1 = 20; 30 x 1 = 30

5. World's Fastest Dog: 41 x 3 = 123; car: 60 x 1 = 60, greyhound: 41 x 2 = 82, dog travels farther

6. Earth Speed: 66,641 x 2 = 133,282; hours in a week: 24 x 7 = 168, 66,641 x 168 = 11,195,688

7. Falcon Flight: 217 x 3 = 651; 217 x 9 = 1,953

8. Fast Cars: 633 x 5 = 3,165; 633 x 8 = 5,064

9. Speedy Spider: 10 x 3 = 30; 10 x 7 = 70

10. French Friends: 254 x 3 = 762; 254 x 9 = 2,286

Answer Key

11. Miles per Gallon: 20 x 19 = 380; 380 x 2 = 760

12. Movie Multiplication: 24 x 60 = 1,440; 1,440 x 90 = 129,600

13. Rocket Science: 41 x 2 = 82; 240,000 x 2 = 480,000

14. Terrific Trains: for both rails: 1.5 x 2 = 3; 2,880 x 2 = 5,760

15. Big Bikes: 15 x 10 = 150; 15 x 109 = 1,635

16. Mountain Math: 29,028 x 8 = 232,224; 29,028 x 40 = 1,161,120

17. Sun Power: 48 x 11 = 528; 48 x 24 = 1,152

18. Floating on Air: 105 x 11 = 1,155; 105 x 24 = 2,520

19. Fastest Planet: 107,030 x 3 = 321,090; 107,030 x 24 = 2,568,720

20. Biplane Beauty: 323 x 12 = 3,876; 323 x 48 = 15,504

21. Cricket Chirping Temperature Gage: (.3 x 60) + 40 = 58; (.3 x 170) + 40 = 91

22. Los Angeles Travel Time: 50 X 1.5 = 75; 65 X 1.5 = 97.5

23. Library Fine: 13 x 3 = 39; 365 x 8 = 2,920

24. Radio Talk: 250 x 35 = 8,750; 310 x 60 = 18,600

25. The Terrific Tin Lizzie: 45 x 7.5 = 337.5; 45 x 11.5 = 517.5

26. Wagon Train Travels: 20 x 3.5 = 70; 20 x 31 = 620

27. Super Stalagmites: 9 x 45 = 405; 16 x 30 = 480

28. One, Two, Three: 150 x 2 = 300; 150 x 3 = 450

29. Kangaroo-Mobile: 10.5 x 4 = 42; 10.5 x 40 = 420

30. Studying Stalactites: 150 x 12 = 1,800; 700 x 0.5 = 350

31. Go, Go, Gorillas!: 7 x 6.5 = 45.5; 7 x 600 = 4,200

32. Big Bugs!: 93 x 9 = 837; 23 x 3.5 = 80.5

33. Harley-Davidson: 90 x 1/4 = 22.5; 90 x 5/8 = 56.25

34. Incredible Iguanas: 14 x 1.75 = 24.5; 3 + (3 x 0.75) = 5.25

35. Big Money: 12 x 42 = 504; 150 x 42 = 6,300

36. Mother of Exiles: 354 x 1/3 = 118; 354 x 2/8 = 88.5

37. Smith River Math: 15 x 1/5 = 3; 30 x 1/3 = 10

38. Mother Camels: 365 x 3 = 1,095; 365 x 7 = 2,555

39. Carrying Camels: 900 x 500 = 450,000; 15,000,000 x 500 = 7,500,000,000

40. Egyptian Displays: 17 x 63 = 1,071; 13 x 63 = 819

Answer Key

41. Dining Elephants: 400 x 4/10 = 160; (600 x 3) x 4/10 = 720

42. Weighing Elephants: 20 x 5,000 = 100,000; 200 x 14,000 = 2,800,000

43. Home Demolition: 40 x 3/4 = 30; 80 x 3/4 = 60

44. Don't Mess with the IRS: 159.78 x 2 = 319.56; 159.78 x 100 = 15,978

45. Viewing Niagara Falls: 20,000 x 60 = 1,200,000; 1,200,000 x 60 = 72,000,000

46. Marvelous Monet: 300 x 2/3 = 200; 300 x 1/2 = 150

47. Look Out, Ants!: 160 x 60 = 9,600; 9600 x 24 = 230,400

48. The Leaning Tower: 3 x 1/20 = 0.15; 10 x 1/20 = 0.5

Division

1. What's in a Whale?: 30 / 6 = 5; varies

2. Wise Water Watching: 840 / 5 = 168; (840 /2) / 5 = 84

3. John T. Scopes: 100 / 5 = 20; 250 / 5 = 50

4. Women in Space: 48 / 3 = 16; 51 / 3 = 17

5. Hairy Math: 525 / 7 = 75; 770 / 7 = 110

6. Typewriter Talent: 880 / 5 = 176; 474 / 3 = 158

7. Big Burrito: 4,460 / 10 = 446; 4,460 / 5 = 892

8. Hamburger Heaven: 5,520 / 3 = 1,840; 5,520 / 6 = 920

9. Michael Math: 504,000 / 7 = 72,000; 504,000 / 9 = 56,000

10. Theater Thinking: 6,000 / 30 = 200; 9,000 / 30 = 300

11. Life in a Rain Forest: 60 / 365 = 0.164; 72 / 365 = 0.197

12. Towering Tree Tops: 200 / 40 = 5; 200 / 12.5 = 16

13. Gorgeous Gemstones: 45.52 / 10 = 4.552; 45.52 / 100 = 0.4552

14. Playing with Pinatas: 18 / 3 = 6; 23 / 3 = 7.6 = 8

15. Busy Bees: 50,000 / 2 = 25,000; 50,000 / 4 = 12,500

16. Cool Constellations: 88 / 8 = 11; 88 / 3 = 29.3

17. Hop on the Hubble: 388 / 97 = 4; 1,440 / 97 = 14.84

18. Traveling by Starlight: 3,000 / 35 = 85.71; 3,000 / 30.5 = 98.36

19. Hello to Halley's Comet: 304 / 76 = 4; 1,000 / 76 = 13.15 = 13

20. Word Count: 4,000 / 250 = 16; 6,375 / 250 = 25.5

21. Sneaky Snakes: 300 / 30 = 10; varies

22. Metric Tessellation: 2.8 / 0.02 = 140; 15 / 0.02 = 750

Answer Key

23. The Unsinkable Ship: 2,200 / 25 = 88; 2,200 / 23 = 95.65 = 96

24. Hop on a Hovercraft: 1,100 / 220 = 5; 11,000 / 220 = 50

25. Slow Sloths: 978 / 2 = 489; 978 / 4 = 244.5

26. The Great Wall of China: 1,500 / 15 = 100; 1,500 / 20.7 = 72.46

27. Feeding a Baby: 28.86 / 6 = 4.81; 28.86 / 8 = 3.6

28. Terrific Turtles: 2,016 / 4 = 504; 2,016 / 215.7 = 9.3

29. Learning Languages: 13 / 8 = 1.625; 13 / 5.5 = 2.363

30. Visiting the Pantheon: 360 / 6 = 60; 360 / 1.5 = 240

31. The Amazing Eiffel: 984 / 90 = 10.93; 984 / 101.5 = 9.69

32. Putting Together a Pinata: 200 / 10 = 20; 225 / 10 = 22.5

33. London Celebrations: 60 / 10 = 6; 60 / 20 = 3

34. The Wright Flyer: 37 / 12 = 3.08; 852 / 59 = 14.44

35. Long Overdue: 2264 / 145 = 15.61; (2,264 / 2) / 145 = 7.80

36. Ellis Island: 12,000,000 / 62 = 193,548; 50,000 / .4 = 125,000

37. Quick Versus Slow: 1 / 0.03 = 33.33; 35 / 70 = 0.5

38. Cock-a-Doodle Dollars: 82 / 30 = 2.73; 150 / 30 = 5

39. Baseball Pitch: 60 ft / (60 x 5,280) = 0.000189;
60 / (95 x 5,280) = 0.0001196

40. Generations: 100 / 30 = 3.33; 2,000 / 30 = 66.67

41. Moon Bicycle Trip: 240,000 / 15 = 16,000; 240,000 / 25 = 9,600

42. Moon Gravity: 200 / 6 = 33.33; varies

Geometry

1. Parking Lot Perimeter: 50 + 50 + 25 + 25 = 150;
100 + 100 + 50 + 50 = 300

2. Pentagon Perimeter: 5 x 2 = 10; 5 x 25 = 125

3. Triangle Perimeter: 6 x 3 = 18; 25 x 3 = 75

4. Hexagon Perimeter: 6 x 5 = 30; 6 x 25 = 150

5. Heptagon Perimeter: 7 x 10 = 70; 7 x 35 = 245

6. Octagon Perimeter: 8 x 15 = 120; 8 x 40 = 320

7. Nonagon Perimeter: 9 x 17 = 153; 9 x 15 = 135

8. Decagon Perimeter: 10 x 6 = 60; 10 x 12 = 120

9. Square Area: 4 x 2 = 8; 4 x 8 = 32

10. Rectangle Area: 45 x 20 = 900; 1,000 x 75 = 75,000